LEEDS
TRAMS AND BUSES

MICHAEL BERRY

AMBERLEY PUBLISHING

First published 2013

Amberley Publishing
The Hill, Stroud
Gloucestershire, GL5 4EP

www.amberley-books.com

Copyright © Michael Berry, 2013

The right of Michael Berry to be identified as the
Author of this work has been asserted in accordance
with the Copyrights, Designs and Patents Act 1988.

ISBN 978 1 4456 1484 7
E-BOOK ISBN 978 1 4456 1490 8

All rights reserved. No part of this book may be
reprinted or reproduced or utilised in any form
or by any electronic, mechanical or other means,
now known or hereafter invented, including
photocopying and recording, or in any information
storage or retrieval system, without the permission
in writing from the Publishers.

British Library Cataloguing in Publication Data.
A catalogue record for this book is available from
the British Library.

Typeset in 9.5pt on 12pt Celeste.
Typesetting by Amberley Publishing.
Printed in the UK.

Leeds and the Transport System

The Early Days

Like many towns in England, early transport in Leeds was provided by horse-drawn stagecoaches which carried passengers and mail between public houses or inns where passengers would disembark for refreshments and rest. In some cases, the local innkeeper was also the bus operator. In the case of Leeds, in 1832 beer seller John Cockill operated cars from the Griffin Inn, West Bar, to Kirkstall, where he was later to become innkeeper. These vehicles ran on Tuesdays and Saturdays to coincide with the markets. Within two years (1834), a passenger-carrying railway service was operating between Leeds and Selby, resulting in, shortly afterwards, a bus service. This new service was to operate from the Leeds & Selby Railway Company offices in Kirkgate to the depot at Marsh Lane Station, this being the Leeds terminus for the railway.

As the population grew, areas such as Roundhay, Chapeltown, Meanwood and Headingley were being provided with some form of bus service. In the case of Headingley and Chapeltown, the residents of the former village decided themselves to form a bus company with which to provide transport to Leeds. This service began three days before the coronation of Queen Victoria, and was operated by cab proprietor John Wood of Headingley. The route consisted of five journeys from the Nags Head (Upperhead Row) to the Three Horseshoes at Far Headingley. With a total distance of around three miles, the trip would take in Woodhouse Lane and Headingley Road. This service, beginning in June 1838, was well used and was possibly the true beginning of suburban transport in the area.

As the horse omnibus era took hold in the 1830s, competition became fierce as cab operators and innkeepers vied for passengers. With the railways also expanding, many operators fell by the wayside and one major competitor, John & William Atkinson, who had been operating a service from the Nags Head to the Spen Lane Tavern at Far Headingley discontinued running stage coaches in 1841, citing railway competition. As bus competition increased, John Wood had tried to fight off an increased operation from the Atkinsons by upgrading his own service, taking in the zoological and botanical gardens, which had become popular attractions for the travelling public. By 1842 he had increased his service to seven journeys a day to coincide with this demand but unfortunately, by February 1845 he had succumbed to the competition and was declared bankrupt.

Headingley had also become the subject of some debate by the 1850s as old, dilapidated carriages continued to run in the area. One disgruntled passenger complained in the *Leeds Mercury* that the buses were late, too small and the conductors unrespectable. All these complaints were ignored and when John Greenwood, a Manchester proprietor, took up the baton by providing newer vehicles for the area, there was a dramatic improvement. Previously, in 1824, John Greenwood had started the United Kingdom's first omnibus service, which ran between Pendleton and Manchester. To cope with passenger traffic in his home town of Manchester, Greenwood's buses were double-deckers with a large seating capacity, a strange sight in Leeds at the time, which highlighted the poor standard of service with which the Leeds public had to contend with. However, modern double-deck cars began to arrive, built by George Starbuck & Co. in Birkenhead and seating forty passengers (twenty inside and twenty outside) in a knifeboard configuration. This arrangement had the passengers sitting back to back on seats placed along the length of the centre of the bus.

With the Municipal Corporations Act of 1835, Leeds became the Municipal Borough of Leeds and had its own elected councillors. The Corporation would invariably take an interest in the local turnpikes and transport system. The Leeds Improvement Act 1866 was passed by Royal Assent on 28 June 1866 and would allow the Corporation to negotiate the purchase of various turnpikes from their trusts, while also providing roadways.

Also in this year, corn and hay merchant William Turton had begun running horse-drawn omnibuses in the Leeds area, building his business up prior to becoming a founding director, and later chairman, of the Leeds Tramways Company from 1872 to 1895.

The Trams

The Leeds Tramways Company was authorised to construct tramway lines in Leeds in 1871, under the Leeds Tramways Order, with the first route opening on 16 September of that year and running from Boar Lane Leeds to the Oak Inn at Headingley. This road later became the A660 and it is still a main bus route today. A year later, Royal Assent was given for the Leeds Tramways Act, and by 1873 William Bulmer from Liverpool was appointed the new manager, while a local man, William Wharam, was appointed as both secretary and treasurer.

Leeds trams came in various guises, from the early horse-drawn vehicles to eventual full electrification (under Corporation ownership), while steam powered vehicles were operated between the two other systems, the first such vehicle being built by the local locomotive building firm of Kitson & Co. in the late 1870s. Another supplier of steam traction engines was Thomas Green, who began building tramway engines in Leeds in 1885 at the Smithfield Foundry. Originally from Newark, Green was probably best known for building in 1855 an early updated design of the lawnmower which had been successful. On moving to Leeds in 1835 he founded the company and operated from Lower Head Row, which was later to become Eastgate. Among his many customers for traction engines were nearby Bradford and Huddersfield Tramways Companies. After exhaustive tests and modifications, the Kitson vehicle was finally put into service in June 1880 and ran on the Wortley route. The passengers were conveyed on adapted horse-drawn trailers. Unfortunately, these were not very popular with the travelling public, due to smoke from the engine billowing over the open top deck.

To correct this flaw the vehicles of 1883, built by Starbuck, had the upper decks covered in at the front and rear, and partially at the sides. The trailer cars were usually built by Milnes or Starbuck and would previously have been horse-drawn. George Starbuck built the first tram cars in Birkenhead in 1871, but by 1886 George Milnes of Manchester had bought the factory and had taken over supplying Leeds and other areas with tramcars. For the Chapletown route, which was normally restricted to single-deck trams, Ashby Railway Carriage of Manchester supplied a trio of lightweight double-deck cars in 1883. These were built to the Eades Reversible system, which enabled the whole car to swivel about its bogie at the terminus without the need for the driver to dismount or even for the horses to be un-hitched. Following a successful experiment using steam traction vehicles, the company added these to their operations and operated both types in unison until its demise on 2 February 1894.

For their part, Leeds Corporation (operating since October 1891) had visions of modernisation and expansion, and, after only twenty-two years in operation, the Leeds Tramways Company was bought out by the Corporation in 1893. The price paid was £112,225 and by 1894 the new company, Leeds Corporation Tramways, was fully in charge of the system and the Tramways Company was no more. Electrification of the system was completed in just seven years and by late 1901 both the horse-drawn trams and the steam vehicles were redundant. An early supplier of electrified cars was the Dick Kerr Company of Kilmarnock and Preston, later bought out by the English Electric Company. Dick Kerr supplied firstly open, then semi-enclosed and later fully enclosed trams to Leeds. Of these, one of the first supplied as fully enclosed, tram number 399 of 1926, is now preserved and running at the Crich Museum.

All through later operations, Leeds used a mixture of ex-Southampton balloon-style and bus-style trams of double-deck build, while Roe of Crossgates supplied single-deck railcars. To negate the act of turning poles at each terminus, Leeds later mainly used the pantograph system on their trams as a means of power collection. Another feature was the ability to reverse the seat backs on trams for the return journey, enabling the passengers to face the direction of travel.

As old stock was withdrawn, the largest series of vehicles supplied for Leeds came in 1926–28, ordered in part by the outgoing administration and partially designed by the new General Manager. Mr William Chamberlain was previously employed as General Manager and Engineer at Oldham Corporation Tramways. Although possibly overseeing the largest influx of new tram stock, Chamberlain was not to rule long at Leeds and by October 1928 he had been offered, and accepted a post at Belfast following the resignation of their acting General Manager. The build order for the new trams numbered 185 cars, with a further seventy-five Pivotals to be built after 1928 by the English Electric Company.

The next appointed General Manager was Robert Lund Horsfield, formerly General Manager of Cardiff Corporation Tramways and with a career based mainly on tramway work behind him. Mr Horsfield hailed originally from Bradford, where at the age of 18 he had joined the Bradford & Shelf Steam Tramway Company, working up to become manager in 1900. The untimely death of Mr Horsfield in 1931, together with the retirement of Alderman Graham Ford, who was the Conservative chairman of the Tramways Committee, was a major pitfall for the tramways. The newly elected chairman, Frederick Leach, and the new General Manager, Mr William Vane Morland, were both anti tramways, Mr Morland being more interested in diesel engines. Mr Morland, who was born in Blackpool, had already presided over the abandonment of the Walsall tramways system in his time as General Manager there, and took over control of the Leeds system on 1 April 1932. In the mid-1930s a select few 'Lance Corporal' trams entered service, running on four-wheel Middleton-type bogies which were designed primarily for use on routes with sharp turns. These vehicles, designed by William Vane Morland, were built at Kirkstall Road Works. Further modernisation followed and in 1949 one of the last new sections of tram track was laid in Britain. This was the Middleton to Belle Isle line on the Middleton Road. Even with the new track opened, and with a further purchase of some ninety Feltham cars in the 1950s, the system was doomed. The 1931 Feltham vehicles were acquired second hand from London Transport and were painted in the red livery of Leeds Corporation. However, the incoming Labour Party was unanimous in the abandonment of the system. The first Leeds tram route ear-marked for abandonment following a meeting by the new administration in 1953 was number 14, running from the Corn Exchange to Half Mile Lane. At this time there were some 379 vehicles of various makes in the tram fleet, while at about the same time the bus fleet consisted of around 416 vehicles, only ten being of single-deck construction. Even though various routes started to be abandoned, due to the renewal needs, costs of infrastructure, and various opponents to the trams, two experimental railcars had already been ordered from Roe in an attempt to modify the elderly fleet. These railcars entered the fleet as late as 1953, when the decision to abandon the system was already in the pipeline, and were painted in an attractive royal purple and cream livery while being finished off with gold leaf lining out. They were designed by General Manager Alexander Black Findlay, who had previously managed Glasgow Corporation Tramways, and were designed along the lines of that city's double-deck Cunarder vehicles. Upon withdrawal in 1957, Tram 601 was destroyed by vandals while sister vehicle 602 has been refurbished and preserved at the Crich Museum. After sixty-eight years, the Leeds Corporation Tramways system was closed down on 7 November 1959, with some of the track from Torre Road Depot being used at the Crich Museum. This left Sheffield as the last city in England operating a tramway, with that system closing a year later. The central 'guided' bus route now used on the A64 York Road is but one of many remains of what was early tram routes around the city.

The Ancillary Fleet

Some Leeds vehicles were still being worked well after their service lives had ended. The Transport Department modified various vehicles for specific requirements from the early days of tram operations through to the more modern motor bus era. For example, five trams were converted as snow brooms for clearing tracks in the winter. Also, a steam tram truck dating from the early 1900s was modified to become a rail grinder by the early 1950s, while an early Chamberlain car was adapted to become an overhead rail derrick. In the case of the motor buses, some early withdrawals had their upper decks modified or partially removed to become tree loppers.

The Motor Buses

The introduction of the first real motor bus operating in Leeds is thought to have come about via a meeting over golf between Councillor R. A. Smithson, then a member of the Headingley Golf Club and chairman of the Tramways Committee, and the incoming General Manager of the Tramways Department, J. B. Hamilton. This was brought about after the re-routing of the Corporation's small ten-seat, horse-drawn bus service in 1904 led to an approach from the golf club to improve the service, and a decision was taken to replace the vehicle with a motor bus. To further enhance the change, the club promised to help finance the scheme by contributing towards any loss the new service would incur for a three year period which would begin in 1906, when a new golf course would be made at Adel.

The Works Sub-Committee was instructed to purchase two motorbuses for service work to run the new route running from the tram terminus at Headingley to Lawnswood Cemetery. After assessment by the Committee, two vehicle chassis were bought from the Rykneild Engine Company in Burton-on-Trent. These were fitted with tram-style bodies by the Leeds Tramways Department staff themselves at their Kirkstall Road Works and entered service in December 1905 and early 1906. The buses carried registration numbers U327/8 and were fitted with thirty-eight garden-style seats while being painted in a light yellow or primrose livery. The top speed of these buses was about 15 mph, and they were used as feeder vehicles to the tram services.

Prior to the mid-1920 orders of vehicles, four 20-seat Guy buses with bodies built by the Tramways Department at Kirkstall Road were used, which had been ordered by General Manager J. B. Hamilton. Mr Hamilton had previously managed Glasgow Corporation Tramways, and became General Manager on 1 April 1902, the last day of steam trams in Leeds. He died in early 1925, after being in charge for twenty-two years. In the period 1925/6, Dennis single-deck buses began to operate around Leeds. The Dennis vehicles were bodied by Strachan & Brown of London and the initial vehicle, UM 873, was the first to adopt the new princess blue and cream livery for Leeds. Subsequent orders were to follow from various suppliers and in 1927 the first Karriers were put into service. These were from a 1926 order of 30-seat single-deck buses to be supplied by Charles H. Roe and were the first Corporation bus bodies supplied by the Leeds firm, while Karrier themselves built locally in Huddersfield. Karrier continued in favour for a time, delivering the WL6 versions, which were 6-wheeled vehicles, again bodied by Roe, on a single-deck or double-deck layout. This was the first British company to instigate this design for passenger transport. Early Leeds buses were fitted with petrol engines, but in 1930 the first diesel (or heavy oil) powered bus was purchased. It was the second of two (the first being petrol engined) supplied by Crossley and fitted with Crossley Condor double-deck bodies, albeit the latter, no. 64 (UB 2375), with a seating capacity of forty-eight, had two fewer seats than the petrol version.

With the beginning of the abandonment of the tram system, the motor buses used for tram replacement came from the pre-war batch of Roe bodied AEC Regents from 1934 which had previously been in storage, and the 1940 batch of Regents numbering 106–25 (of which HUM 401, fleet no. 106, built in 1940, is preserved at Keighley Bus Museum) as no new vehicles had been purchased. HUM 401 had been withdrawn in 1952 but was restored to service as a tram replacement vehicle, following a repaint.

Many Leeds buses over the years appeared on display at the Commercial Motor Show, and these entered service with gold lining to distinguish this fact. The 1948 exhibit was to be another first for Leeds, as AEC Regent III MNW 600 was displayed. The bus, built by Roe, entered service as no. 600 and was the first 8-foot-wide bus bought by the Department. All previous orders were for the 7 foot 6 inch body designs.

Early liveries from before 1948, with variants of blue or blue and cream, were carried through to the first motorbuses while dark green with a pale green band became the norm for the fleet after 1952. The last buses delivered in the blue livery were a batch of twenty-five AEC Regent III vehicles in 1950, built by Roe. These vehicles were registered NUB 601–25, carried fleet numbers accordingly, and were quickly repainted in the new two-tone green livery. This livery was used in conjunction with the full destination blind, which the fleet carried until 1968, by which time all vehicles had the new destination blinds fitted. However, in the early 1960s the livery was changed to light green around the windows with the introduction of a less informative destination blind. The livery was changed again to be reversed with the purchasing of the Department's first dual-door, one-man-operated double-deck buses, bought in 1968, which, as with earlier practices, were built by Roe to a design by the Leeds General Manager of the day, this time Thomas Lord. Early one-man operations had begun in Leeds with the purchase of a batch of single-deckers in 1962 for the no. 9 Ring Road service. These were AEC Reliances carrying 41-seat dual-door bodies built locally by Roe, but painted in the original livery of dark green with light green relief around the windows. Subsequent repaints led to this livery being reversed in later years. Also in this year, the Department's first and only batch of front-entrance, front-engine buses was purchased. This was a small batch of Roe-bodied Daimler CVG/6 70-seat buses which were bought specifically to run the joint Bradford route in conjunction with that undertaking's AEC Regent V buses. In October 1960 General Manager Alexander Black Findlay, who had bitterly opposed the abandonment of the tram system, retired due to ill health and in February 1961 Thomas Lord, who had been General Manager of Barrow in Furness since 1949, took control of Leeds City Transport. In 1964 Thomas Lord proposed the introduction of radio-telephone units for the buses – a new concept in England but one which had been introduced abroad. The trial would be for an initial twelve vehicles to be fitted with the units, and these could then be in touch with the Swinegate headquarters in regard to road and service operations. The Transport Department's first rear-engine bus purchases also took place that year and were Daimler Fleetlines, built again by Charles H. Roe of Crossgates, Leeds. A year later, the first rear-engine Leyland Atlanteans arrived, this time bodied by Weymann, unusually. Roe was always the preferred coachbuilder choice for Leeds buses, although MCW, Park Royal and Weymann had provided vehicles for the Department. While the Department operated Leyland, Daimler and early Crossleys, Leeds was also an ardent AEC Regent operator from the early 1930s, with the last versions of this type of vehicle entering service in 1966. In 1960, an order for fourteen Regent V type buses, destined to be made by Roe, was transferred to MCW at Birmingham. These were unique in as much as they were the Department's last vehicles with exposed radiators, and had 30-foot rear-entrance bodies, a design not used anywhere else on this chassis. The first of this batch of vehicles, 3910 UB, was featured in the 1963 film *This Sporting Life*, which starred Richard Harris and Rachel Roberts. An early identification of a Leeds City Transport motorbus must be the unpainted bonnets on the vehicles. This was a characteristic of the Department for many years, and was merely designed as a measure to protect the paintwork (or lack of it), from the engineering Department's greasy hands!

In an effort to maximise private hire work, a dual purpose coach was bought in 1965. This was bodied by Roe on an AEC Reliance chassis and entered the fleet as no. 10. The vehicle was registered ANW 710C and was built to carry thirty-seven passengers. Towards the end of that year, the last batch of rear entrance buses to be purchased by Leeds arrived from Roe on the AEC Regent V chassis. These were registered DUM 964–973C in 1965 and ENW 974–983D for the early 1966 deliveries.

Following the 1970 Earls Court Motor Show, some annoyance was shown among the local press as Leeds turned its back on British bus manufacturers in favour of German-built Mercedes Benz vehicles for its first real purchase of mini-buses. The first town to operate this system, these vehicles were 13-seater vehicles based on the van chassis. The mini-buses introduced a new livery, ivory with a wide dark green dark green band, for this section of the fleet and were used primarily for a dedicated route, the no. 401 shoppers' service operating on the pedestrianised area of Commercial Street and Bond Street. A batch of six vehicles was delivered, numbering YUA 530/5J consecutively, and were given fleet numbers 30–5. They carried Deansgate bodies, and entered service in late 1970. Two years later, another attempt at 'Shoppers' Specials' saw the short lived introduction of the experimental Morrison Electricar, a firm more noted for many years for making battery-powered delivery vans and milk floats. This was one of two electric minibuses, with bodywork built by Willowbrook to their B9F design, which could carry up to twenty-six passengers at a top speed of approximately 25 miles per hour. It was fitted to a Leyland Redline chassis, registered CWO 516K, which was built in Tredegar, Monmouth, by Leyland Electricals, a subsidiary of British Leyland and Hawker Siddeley. It was painted in an orange livery with a white front, and was commissioned by the Department of Industry. It was first used on 10 April 1972 for route 403 car park duty, but later transferred to the route 401 shoppers' service. The power output was estimated at about 35 miles' service time, and after these trials the vehicles were deemed unsatisfactory for the city. It completed its final journey on 27 July of the same year and was transferred to other areas of the country for further trials.

On New Year's Eve 1976, the last rear-entrance bus ran in Leeds. This was a Roe-bodied Daimler CVG6/30 (7514 UA), 30 feet in length, which began service as a tram replacement vehicle on the Halton route on 7 December 1959. Another vehicle from this batch, no. 502 (7502 UA), had been placed on loan to nearby Huddersfield Corporation in 1962, for evaluation for trolleybus replacements. Following the emergence of the West Yorkshire PTE on 1 April 1974, new vehicles were still being delivered to Leeds and various towns throughout West Yorkshire in department livery. In the case of Leeds, these buses were of the reversed two-tone green one-man livery, albeit with red wheels, although the words Metro Leeds were later to appear on the vehicles. The last vehicle to be delivered in Leeds City livery was Leyland Atlantean SUG 591M in March 1974, just two weeks prior to the formation of the PTE. Shortly after the PTE formation the Leeds Seacroft garage was closed down, and on 5 October 1978 the last bus remaining in Leeds City Transport livery, Leyland Atlantean 481 (DUA 481K), was repainted into Metro/PTE Verona green and the Leeds identity was gone. Leeds had coinciding fleet and registration numbers on their buses from 1947, a system quite widely used within bus companies for ease of identification. However, as ownership was changed to within the PTE jurisdiction, this system was abandon after 1974.

This is but a brief condensed resumé of Leeds City and its very complicated and varied transport system, which cannot possibly be totally explained fully within this one volume. A much more concentrated look can be found, among other places, in the Leeds Transport Historical Society volumes by J. Soper.

A well laden three-horse omnibus is seen around 1901 outside the Bay Horse Hotel in Hunslet, near the corner of Woodhouse Hill Terrace. The owners were Mr J. T. Bean & Son, with what is thought to be Mr John Thomas Bean holding the reins at the centre of the upper seat in this picture.

An early British Thomson-Houston (BTH) Tramways single-deck vehicle at Sheepscar Junction. The system at that time used cross wire suspension lines and ran on 4 feet 8½ inch gauge rails. This picture is un-dated.

Kirkstall Road Works at Leeds was the hub of the Tramways operations. This shot typifies the scale of operations there, which included the construction of tram bodies. On view is balcony car 225, which was the first electric tram to run to Horsforth, on 11 May 1906. To the right is a fully enclosed tram.

A large crowd gathered as the Mayor of Morley, Alderman Sam Rhodes, drove new tramcar 238 on its inaugural journey to Morley on 5 July 1911, with his guests the Lord and Lady Mayoress of Leeds and members of the Morley Town Council.

A line-up of early open balcony cars with boom pick up arms waits at Elland Road. Mr John Baillie Hamilton, then manager at Leeds, designed these cars, which entered service in 1911/12 but were later converted to enclosed tops.

A rare nearside street shot of a very busy North Lane, as a motorbus on route 47 (Old Farnley) passes a procession of trams while a car tries to weave around the trams.

This very rare mid-1930s shot in Hawksworth Road shows 224, one of 100 Horsfield trams (155–254) built by Brush on Peckham P35 trucks, in 1931 with the early lined out fleet number in view and in the blue and cream livery. Leeds trams did not travel outside the city boundary and by 17 January 1949 this length of track was abandoned, terminating instead at Kirkstall Abbey.

Waiting time at Half Mile Lane on route 14 to Corn Exchange is Horsfield tram 153, which was eventually scrapped in June 1959. The Horsfield tram behind appears to be in the all-blue livery, which was not widely used among the fleet.

The ascending tram on route 17 (Halton) prepares to leave the White Horse on York Road (now the A64). Even though the width of the road has not altered, most of the buildings have now gone due to re-development.

On special duty at Haddon Place is Middleton bogie car 255, in the pre-war blue livery. This was the first of seventeen such vehicles built in 1933, designed by General Manager W. Vane Morland and built by the Tramways Department at Leeds.

Another Middleton bogie car, number 257 of these 70-seat vehicles (thirty lower saloon, forty upper saloon) which were finally withdrawn between 1956 and 1957. This winter scene is on the Ring Road at Belle Isle.

While from the same batch, car no. 258 carries the alternate livery on the 19 route to Lower Wortley, and is pictured here at Stanningley. These vehicles had been designed to cope with the Middleton section of track, where the downhill section had been the cause of some accidents.

While of the same batch, car 258 carries the alternate livery on the 19 route to Lower Wortley, and is pictured here at Stanningley. These vehicles had been designed to cope with the Middleton section of track where the downhill section had been the cause of some accidents.

On the Middleton circular route 12, Feltham car 506 passes the former Middleton Colliery on the line sanctioned in the Leeds Corporation Act of 1919 to extend the Tramway from Dewsbury Road to Middleton.

The scene is a foggy Harehills Lane, Leeds, with a pair of Felthams en route. These vehicles were built by the Union Construction Company (UCC) at Feltham, Middlesex, with forty-two/twenty-eight seating.

Feltham car 505 is seen at the Halton terminus on route 22, Temple Newsham, with a Horsfield car on route 20.

Built by Brush to a Horsfield design, car 187 of 1931 stands tall next to ex-London Feltham 501 of the same year. The Feltham, numbered 2099 in the capital's fleet, was the first to be acquired, in 1949, and ran until closure of the system in 1959 before being returned to London to be preserved at Clapham Museum.

Heading through Kirkgate on the single track is Feltham 523, in-bound to the Corn Exchange. A brace of Horsfield trams can be seen following.

This former London Feltham is seen on the wide central tramway at York Road, Killingbeck. This area has now been redeveloped to include a huge Asda retail store.

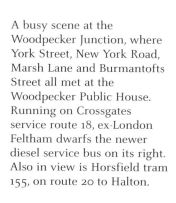

A busy scene at the Woodpecker Junction, where York Street, New York Road, Marsh Lane and Burmantofts Street all met at the Woodpecker Public House. Running on Crossgates service route 18, ex-London Feltham dwarfs the newer diesel service bus on its right. Also in view is Horsfield tram 155, on route 20 to Halton.

CROSS FLATTS
9

299

Car 299, seen at Swinegate, is from a batch of ex-Southampton 1930 cars bought in 1949. Unlike the Felthams from London, these vehicles did not reign long in the city, with some being scrapped only four years after delivery.

Tram 359, one of the early 1920s open balcony vehicles (later converted to enclosed balcony), is decorated to commemorate the Festival of Britain in 1951 and is seen in Stoneybeck Lane.

Although it is not clear what occurred at this Dewsbury Road (Crossflats) scene, it does show the chaos that a derailment could cause to the system as the official in the centre of the picture takes notes regarding the damage to the Feltham car. The David Tomlinson/Diana Dors film advertised dates this shot to around 1953.

Horsfield tram 242, on the number 12 Middleton route, is seen at the former Parkside Crossing, an area which is now part of the M1.

Horsfield tram 156 on the number 20, Corn Exchange, is seen at Crossgates, Leeds, with Feltham 531 following.

Horsfield car 160 on route 2 passes the Woodman Hotel, Leeds, on route 2 for Moortown. This vehicle was decorated tram 10, which ran on the final day procession to Temple Newsham. (*Malcolm King Collection*)

At the top of Kirkgate stood the Penny Bank Building, at the junction of York Street and Kirkgate, with an inward bound Feltham car heading up towards Vicar Lane while an outbound 195 Horsfield car heads out on a 17 Crossgates service.

A busy scene at Torre Road as Horsfield tram 165 passes the premises of Stokes & Dalton Ltd, which specialised in 'spice foods', rusks and cornflakes. The Torre Road garage was opened in 1938 by Lord Stamp of the London, Midland & Scottish Railway and was once home to some eighty trams and 112 buses.

Passengers rush to board Horsfield tram 200 on a wet day in Kirkgate as alongside is parked a Department van. Another popular advertisement on Leeds buses and trams was of course for the local brewer Joshua Tetley, which was founded in Leeds in 1822.

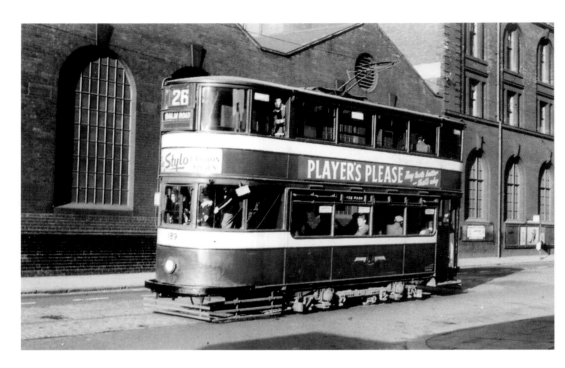

A tramcar of the same batch, meanwhile, carries a full upper destination box to indicate route 26 for Balm Road as it passes through Swinegate. As mentioned in the text previously, Balm Road was once the home of the RET Company, who had earlier supplied the initial trackless cars for Leeds.

As Horsfield car 156 rests at the Crossgates terminus, prepared for the inbound journey to the Corn Exchange, a youngster makes the most of the platform as a seat.

Horsfield tram 177, from the 1931 batch of Brush bodies, passes the Central Bus Station, filled with its diesel counterparts, as the system's demise nears.

This ex-Sunderland car entered the tram fleet as number 600 and was re-bodied by LCT in 1953. (*Malcolm King Collection*)

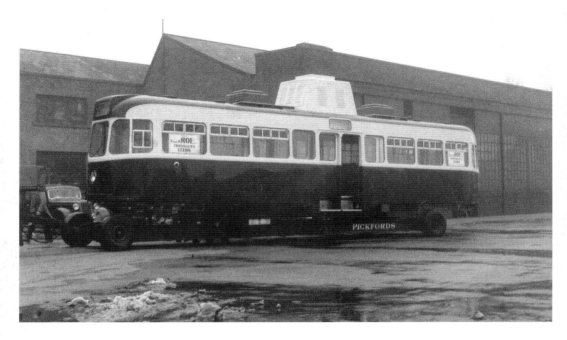

It was common practice for coachbuilders to have their products photographed at their premises at the end of production and Charles H. Roe of Crossgates, Leeds, was no exception. One of the two experimental single deck trams from 1953 is being prepared for delivery. One of these vehicles (602) is preserved at Crich Tramway Museum.

An obvious counter-productive measure was the lack of tracks for delivery purposes, leading to hauliers being called in to transport the trams. Here, the end product is on board a Pickford's low-loader trailer.

The last day procession of trams was numbered 1 to 10. Seats on these were allocated by a ballot system and vehicles 1 and 10 were appropriately adorned with lights. Tram 1 prepares to leave Swinegate Depot with a standing-room only load on 7 November 1959.

Horsfield trams 186 and 200 form part of the final day procession. For those who lost out on a trip on the decorated vehicles, any tram would do for that final trip. Trams 1–5 went to Crossgates, while 6–10 ran to Temple Newsham.

Seen leaving Swinegate, Pickfords Scammel Tractor unit M2092 (YXD 552) begins the trip back to London with Feltham 501 for its future preservation.

Car R2 of the ancillary fleet, which was used for transporting stores around the system and was adapted from BTH tram 73A built in 1937. (*Malcolm King Collection*)

Although not a Leeds ancillary vehicle, this Leyland Beaver tow-truck is captured with an early Roe bodied Regent, heading through Austhorpe for the breakers yard.

The Leeds ancillary fleet consisted of varying vehicles, some of which were further converted for private enterprises. Former fleet number 142 (ANW 685), an example of the 56-seat Roe bodied Regents supplied in 1934, is seen here converted to a tar-spreader.

AEC Regent II DUB 949 from the 1936 batch (as seen on page 36) on duty at the construction of the Middleton Depot after being converted to a gravel wagon in 1953. It was the last vehicle of that order and was withdrawn in 1970.

A nearside view of a converted AEC Regent gravel wagon heading through East End Park.

Another conversion was UG 6308, which was fitted with a gritting hopper and is seen here at the Middleton Depot.

Not what it seems! This breakdown tender (UB 7931) is actually a Dennis chassis, fitted with an AEC radiator, which normally operated from Torre Road garage and lasted well into PTE operations. It has been preserved and is currently awaiting restoration. (*M. Berry Collection*)

Leeds City 179 was a converted AEC Regent dating from 1935. The original Roe (H30/26R) body was adapted for tree lopping duties in 1955. In the background stands RNW 301, one of the ten Roe H33/25R body Leyland PD2/14s delivered in 1953. (*M. Berry Collection*)

Leeds AEC Matador breakdown tender MUB 647 in the later green livery rescues JUB 591, a Brush bodied Daimler CWA6 (H30/26R) dating from 1946. The Matador was acquired via the armed forces in 1949, and is currently preserved in Metro livery at the Keighley Bus Museum.

Another vehicle in the ancillary fleet was this Bedford OB tower wagon with crew cabin. Although no history can be found for this vehicle, the bus behind reveals it to be in some form of use long after the trams had disappeared. (*Malcolm King Collection*)

A Bradford registered Leyland Beaver fitted with a Holmes 600 jig and carrying the Department Trade Plate 0619 U rescues an AEC Swift. (*Malcolm King Collection*)

Leeds HUM 401 had a busy and varied career. Supplied by Roe in 1940 as fleet no. 106, after withdrawal from service work in 1952 it was re-instated as a tram replacement vehicle. In 1956 it was re-numbered as no. 1 in the learner fleet. It is seen in its later two-tone green livery while on National Savings week.

One of the 1940 batches of Regents (HUM 406) in the early version of green livery at Sovereign Street yard on learner duty.

Three AEC Regents from the learner fleet rest at the Preston shed at Torre Road. HUM 401, dating from 1940, has been preserved in the blue livery at Keighley Bus Museum.

By the time the Leyland Titan PD2/11 vehicles had begun entering the learner fleet, a new dedicated dark green and white livery had been adopted. UUA 207, dating from 1955, is now in private preservation in standard Leeds livery. (*Malcolm King Collection*)

This early picture shows the variety of vehicles used by the system for Elland Road football ground service. The 48-seater Crossley Condors to the left of the shot were acquired new in the early 1930s but averaged only five years' service. One of the ANW-registered Regents to the right, no. 139 (ANW 682), is preserved at the Keighley Bus Museum.

In 1935, Leeds took delivery of this one-off Weymann 'Streamliner' AEC Regent, with a 7.7 litre diesel engine, a pre-select gearbox, and fluid flywheel. It entered the fleet as 201 and was registered CNW 902. In 1949 it was sent on loan to Chiswick (London) but by then had been converted to a standard half-cab vehicle. (*Scott Blackman collection/ R. Marshall*)

Parked in Dunisthorpe Street Works near Hunslet, Leeds, AEC Regent II DUB 940 from 1936 (220) had suffered substantial rear end damage, as seen in this shot. It was subsequently repaired and finally withdrawn in 1950. Between 1953 and 1958, it worked for the Electricity Board as staff transport.

From the 1938 batch, fleet number 276 stands in the Central Bus Station awaiting departure for North Lane in yet another livery variation. A selection of these buses was later used for driver training duties in 1956, but they were finally withdrawn in 1963. The early Roe products were fitted with half-drop windows, and also evident is the raised waist rail which was a feature of their vehicles.

An early Regent, later used as tram replacements, in Eastgate, while in the background stands the factory of Henry Thorne, who was a sweet manufacturer in nearby Edward Street.

AEC Regent GUA 794, from a batch delivered in 1938, carries a Roe H31/25R body and is seen at Compton Road. The initial green livery with the narrow band was first introduced in 1952.

GNW 707, a Leyland Tiger TS8 with Roe bodywork which dates from 1938, is seen at Wortley.

Standing outside Bramley Depot is one of the Roe B36R bodied Leyland Tigers, which were bought primarily to cover two routes not accessible by double-deckers.

Seen on special duty at Headingley is JUB 587, a Daimler CWA6 built in 1945 to a utility design by Brush of Loughborough. A later similar batch was re-bodied in 1955, as in the next view.

Passing through Vicar Lane on a circular route is JUG 111, one of three from a batch of nine such Daimler CWA6 utilities purchased in 1946 that were re-bodied in 1955 using, strangely, these bodies originally fitted to the AEC Regents from 1934. Even after re-bodying, this batch began to be withdrawn just twelve months later.

Although these buses were more normally associated with routes 67 (Dib Lane) and 68 (Foundry Lane) from the bus station, this Crossley H30/26R bodied Crossley of 1948 was one of a batch of twenty and is seen here in Bond Street on route 15 to Seacroft.

One of the 1948 all-Crossley vehicles enters Eastgate past the Quarry Hill flats, which was made famous by the television programme *Queenie's Castle*.

Although the manager at time of this picture was Thomas Lord, the delivery date of these two Leyland PS1/Roe B36R buses goes back to 1948, the time that W. Vane Morland was coming to the end of his term as General Manager and A. B. Findlay was about to take over a year later. (*Malcolm King Collection*)

Roe bodied LUA 426 from 1947 is seen at Middleton Ring Road on service 29. Of this batch, sister vehicle 423 was sent to Halifax Joint Committee for a short time to help cover for a delay in delivery of new vehicles.

The following batch (fleet numbers 431–99), delivered in 1948, had basically similar bodies but minus the famous Roe waist rail which previously had been fitted to the Department's buses since 1932.

A year later, Roe became part of the ACV group and built this body to the design of Park Royal, which was also a member of the group. It was again fitted to an AEC Regent III 9612E chassis; this was the only vehicle built by Roe to this design.

On Vicar Lane, Leeds, is LNW 524, one of ten (522–31) Daimler CVD/6s with Brush H30/26R bodywork, bought new in 1948/9. They were withdrawn ten years later.

This Hyde Park Corner scene is ideal as the front and rear aspect of the 1948 Brush bodied Daimlers are in view. On the outward 60 circular is LNW 525, while on the opposite side of the road stands sister vehicle LNW 523.

Standing in Sovereign Street Yard are a brace of Crossleys (714 and 717), and AEC Regents 423 and 429.

Under the radiator covers at Bramley Depot yard are two of the 1938 Leyland Tigers and NNW 353, one of the sixty Leyland PD2/1s bought in 1949/50.

Between 1949/50, a large order of sixty Leyland PD2/1s which were fitted with Leyland H30/26R bodies arrived. One such vehicle is seen here at the Central Bus Station in the two-tone blue livery.

Despite the efforts of Aveling Porter Road Roller E5351, NNW 382 of the 1949/50 intake of the Leyland bodied vehicles makes decent headway at the Corn Exchange.

Pictured at the Headrow is NNW 360, an all-Leyland PD2/1 repainted in the green livery.

Roadside repairs as NNW 340 of the Leyland fleet has tyre troubles on Infirmary Street.

At the junction of York Road and Lupton Avenue is Leyland 367, a comparison picture with the scene on page 23.

The all-Leyland buses of 1949/50 were the mainstay of the Rodley and Halton Moor route 54 throughout their lives. Here, NNW 375 (375) is seen at Halton Moor. These vehicles were also among the last to carry the full destination blinds.

AEC Regent III MUG 464, one of the twenty-five of this type supplied in 1949 with Roe H31/25R bodywork, is seen at Hyde Park.

NUB 616, a 1950 Roe H31/25R-bodied AEC Regent III, is at the stop at Hyde Park Corner as JUM 576, a Roe-bodied Daimler CWD/6 of 1946 vintage, passes on the 60 Circular route.

Passing through Swinegate is ONW 630, a 1950 AEC Regent III with Roe H31/25R bodywork. It was from one of the first 8-foot-wide production batch delivered to the Department.

At Rockingham Street bus station is Roe-bodied JUG 622, a Leyland PD1 with a Roe H31/25R body which dates from 1946. Eight years later, the AEC Regent displays some refinement from the builder, including better ventilators and a chromed cab window frame. Also just visible is the Limited Stop sign, situated adjacent to the cab, which was illuminated to show when the bus was on a semi-express service and would only use designated bus stops.

Among the last AEC Regent IIIs to enter service for Leeds was TNW 749, a 1954 example built by Roe with H33/25R bodywork. A similar batch was supplied by Metro-Cammell (page 67) in the same year. Leeds 749 is seen parked at Austhorpe on service 9.

Sovereign Street, which runs between Neville Street and Swinegate, has (like most of the city) been host to some re-development. However, the Stembridge building at the corner of Concordia Street in the background remains basically unchanged, although it is now used as an office complex. A line-up of Roe-bodied vehicles awaits their journey to Elland Road football ground.

During 1954/5, a batch of single decks arrived, split between AEC Reliance, Leyland Tiger Cub and Guy Arab chassis. TUA 29 (29), from the batch of three Leyland Tiger Cubs, dates from 1955 and this picture shows to great effect the body layout of these vehicles. (*Malcolm King Collection*)

The Roe body designs on these vehicles were basically the same, to a B34C+24 standard design. TUA 32, from the batch of three Reliances, is seen at Meanwood.

This offside view of TUA 35 at North Lane, Headingley, shows little external difference between the three groups of vehicles. The Guy Arabs were fitted with the 5LW engine.

The 1955 batch of fifteen Leyland PD2/11s built by Roe were to be the penultimate vehicles to be fitted with an offside staircase window, which had previously been a feature of this coachbuilder. Two of these vehicles have been preserved.

Sister vehicle UUA 203 is seen on Church Street, Hunslet, with the remains of the tram lines and setts yet to be covered over. This area has now been vastly re-developed. The Department bought thirty Titan chassis in the 1950s, which were delivered in two batches.

In 1955 the Corporation bought twenty Leyland Titan PD2/11 chassis, the first fifteen being bodied by Roe. The final five, however, were built by MCW to their Orion design. UUA 217 in the fleet is seen loading at Briggate.

In City Square, on Beeston service 1, is a 1956 Daimler CVG6 with a Metro-Cammell H33/28R body.

The subsequent batch of Daimlers with Orion bodies from Metro-Cammell for some reason lacked the upper saloon front ventilators, as indicated on YNW 561 on Woodhouse Lane.

A pre-delivery shot of WUA 762, one of the 1956 AEC Regent V buses supplied by Charles H. Roe of Crossgates, Leeds.

On the 61 Eastgate service, WUA 767 is seen at Albion Place. This area is now mainly pedestrianised.

The crew of WUA 778 take a rest at the City Square. The rolled up radiator blind was a common fitment on Leeds buses.

The backdrop is East End Park for fleet no. 839 (WUA 839), complete with gold lining out indicating that it had been a Show Exhibit. Also in this view can be seen the Roe staircase quarter window which was fitted at this time.

The tram tracks are still in evidence as Regent Vs head the line up at the Preston Shed, Torre Road.

A later Leeds Transport line up for football ground service. Note the complete contrast in the differing body styles between the Roe product from 1958 (1903 NW) and the box like Metro-Cammell body of the earlier Daimler CVG6 (H33/28R), dating from 1956. The AEC was from the new wider (8 feet) batch of MD2RA chassis (H33/29R) of 1958.

5221 NW, the initial bus of an impressive delivery of seventy-one such Leyland Titan PD3/5 buses, and a 1958 Earls Court Motor Show exhibit is a sad image of its former glory.

Leyland PD3/5, 258 (5258 NW) of 1958/9 is seen passing the Middleton Arms on the no. 12 Corn Exchange route. It was fitted with a Roe H38/32R body. Of this group, 5228 NW (a former learner bus) is preserved and undergoing restoration at Halifax.

One of the first 8-foot-wide AEC Regent Vs which had been built by Roe for 1958 delivery is pictured at Beeston.

Four of the 1939/40 AEC Regents are parked at the Skelton Grange Power Station while operating for the Central Electrical Generating Board in 1959.

This immaculate 70-seat Roe bodied Daimler CVG6LX/30 of 1959 at Thorpe Lane, Middleton, was the first delivered of a batch of thirty. These vehicles were also among the first 30-foot buses the Department bought, hence the wide five-bay body construction.

At the end of its Departmental use, no. 712 of this batch was donated to the French town of Lille (twinned with Leeds) by the PTE in April 1977. It was repainted and carried both Leeds City and Metro PTE crests. On the offside of the vehicle was this notice in English, with the French translation fitted to the nearside panels. (*Malcolm King*)

The Corporation loaned no. 502 to neighbouring Huddersfield Corporation in April 1962 for trolleybus replacement evaluation purposes, where it was used extensively on their Golcar route. The exercise was successful and orders were placed for both Corporation and Joint Committee fleets. The bus is seen here at the former Huddersfield Bus Station.

Also delivered in 1959 were these AEC Reliances with Roe bodies, seen here on the Wortley 45 route at Austhorpe.

Unusually, the complete order for these vehicles consisted of just two buses, numbers 37 and 38. The second of that delivery is seen on a private duty.

An inbound 56 bus looks well laden, as a relatively new 3920, one of the unique exposed radiator AEC Regent Vs dating from 1960, leaves Leeds on the Lawnswood route. These buses were nicknamed 'washing machines' by public and crew alike due their excessive vibration and were not well liked. Sister vehicle 916 is preserved and in private ownership. (*M. Berry Collection*)

The 'Clippie' poses with 3915 UB, a 1960 Regent V, as the crew pause on the number 6 Belle Isle service. These high capacity buses were regular servants of this route.

Leeds continued to loan out un-required elderly buses to other operators. Leyland PD2/1 of 1950, together with other Leeds vehicles, is pictured in Harrogate Bus Station, on hire to the West Yorkshire Road Car Company, probably for vehicle shortage relief for that company.

Leeds Central Bus Station, with the massive Quarry Hill flats as a backdrop, is seen from the railway embankment near the grounds of St Peter's church. In evidence are a variety of Leeds Transport and West Riding Automobile Company buses.

Roe-bodied Leyland PD1 JUG 631 (331) of 1946 vintage is pictured at the Corn Exchange bound for Rodley. Two years after purchase, it was fitted with a Leyland o600 engine to help with its performance on this route. It was finally withdrawn in July 1962. Although still fitted with the early destination blind, 331 is seen in the later livery.

In the early 1960s more light green relief was added around the lower window bays, together with a far less comprehensive destination blind, as shown on this Daimler CVG6 at North Lane.

The buildings are cleaner, and the shop owners and lower façades have changed but otherwise to the all-Leyland bus travelling up The Headrow in this mid-1960s shot, the road is the same. The building showing 'That Riviera Touch' now shows clothes as it has become a Primark store.

The later livery, which featured more light green relief, on the 1956 Daimler CVG6 compares with the earlier more drab livery which adorns the 1948 Crossley at Seacroft.

The driver of PUA 652 poses at North Lane, Headingley, in front of his steed, an AEC Regent III, one of only six purchased with Weymann bodies in 1952 in conjunction with orders of the same build from Roe. These vehicles were of the pre-Orion design.

Another variation of the fleet was these AEC Regent III vehicles with Metro-Cammell H33/25R bodies dating from 1954. These bodies were more normally seen on Daimler or Leyland chassis.

Of the three most prominent chassis manufacturers in the fleet (the other being AEC), the exposed radiator Leyland looks somewhat dated when passed by the Daimler with the concealed design, even though both bodies were built by Roe.

AEC Regent ONW 626 of the early batch of 8-footers is seen at the doorway of Hunslet Depot.

Middleton Depot is the lonely setting for 5251 NW, although the actual bulk order for this particular batch totalled seventy-one vehicles. All built by Roe, these 70-seater Leyland PD3/5s, delivered in 1958/9 for tram replacement, had air brakes and Pneumocyclic gearboxes and were the largest single order for exposed radiator PD3s. Of this batch, 5280 NW is preserved at Ensign Bus.

Leeds Transport on film. The first vehicle of the 1960 batch of Regent Vs (3910 UB) was picked for film duty in 1963, when it appeared in the film *This Sporting Life*, which starred Richard Harris and Rachel Roberts.

In 1962 a batch of five Roe body front entrance Daimler CVG6LX/30 vehicles were purchased. These were to be the Department's only front-engine, front-entrance buses in the fleet and were bought specifically for the joint Bradford 72 route. Two of these vehicles (572 and 574) have been preserved. 572 CNW is seen in Stanningley Road.

In 1962, Leyland Titan PD3A/2s with St Helens-style fibre glass fronts were introduced. These were bodied by Weymann (H39/31R). Of this batch, 319 DUA is seen at Kirkstall on the Crossgates service.

A mixed bag at Middleton garage includes 317 DUA, a 1962 Weymann-bodied Leyland; WUA 790 from the 1956 Roe-bodied Regent Vs; and a Leyland PD3/5 from the 1958/9 delivery.

The new look front Leylands now compared well with their Daimler counterparts, although the box-like tapered design of the MCW Orion body on the Leyland still let the overall effect down, as this Roe-bodied Daimler shows when passing it at Kirkstall.

On Middleton Ring Road is 584 FUM, a Daimler CVG6LX/30 with Roe body which was new in 1963.

322 CNW represents the next delivery of Leyland PD3A/2 Weymann vehicles, which were delivered in October 1963.

In 1964, Leeds took delivery of these AEC Reliance 2MU3RA Roe-bodied single deck buses. They were fitted with dual-door 41-seat bodies. 44 KUA picks up outside the Star & Garter, near Kirkstall.

AEC Reliance 46 KUA from 1964 stands at Kirkstall Lane on the short-lived dedicated 222 Park and Ride service. After this batch, Leeds were to begin ordering AEC Swifts for its single deck fleet.

This late picture of LUA 437 of 1948 shows a new AEC Regent chassis/cab cowl alongside waiting for body fitment. (*Malcolm King Collection*)

The first concealed radiator 30-foot AEC Regent Vs arrived in 1964, with 949 JUB. Some of these vehicles were later to find further employment with Tyne & Wear Corporation after withdrawal from Leeds. 952 JUB from this batch is preserved with the Lincolnshire Vintage Vehicle Society in Lincoln.

The first rear engine bus in Leeds in 1964 was this Daimler Fleetline, 101 LNW. As was almost the norm by now, it was a Roe product and a Commercial Motor Show exhibit. It received the usual Roe finishing touches, including gold lining out and unusually light green relief around the upper deck windows. Another first for this bus was forced air ventilation.

The remainder of the delivery looked a lot more basic than the show model. Gone were the wrap around windscreen and the twin headlights, sliding ventilators were fitted and it was back to basics with the livery.

Differing Daimlers. A Roe-bodied Atlantean of 1964 passes a tin-fronted rear-entrance MCW Orion-bodied CVG6 of 1955/6.

The next delivery of rear engine vehicles was yet another change for Leeds. The 1965 buses were built by Weymann with H41/29F seating, this time on Leyland Atlantean PDR1/1 Mk 2 chassis. The second numerically registered vehicle (CUB 332C) is seen on the 16 Bramley route at Gipton. The first of this batch, CUB 331C, is preserved in private ownership at Keighley Bus Museum.

The first coach bought by the Department for tour work was ANW 710C, a 1965 AEC Reliance with Roe C37F bodywork which was painted in this attractive two-tone green and cream livery. (*Malcolm King Collection*)

This 1965 Regent negotiates Becket Street corner in the early 1970s, past the Dock Green Inn on Stanley Road, which still stands today.

ENW 980D of the 1966, and final, batch of Roe deliveries of AEC Regent V vehicles is seen at Gipton. The Regent V chassis accounted for some 204 orders for Leeds, all but fourteen (the 1960 MCW batch) of which were built by Roe. No. 980, with a H39/31R body, was finally withdrawn on 20 December 1975 and was eventually bought by the Leeds Regent Preservation Group. It is currently at Keighley.

Kirkgate Abattoir in New York Lane is the backdrop as 580 CNW, a Daimler CVG6LX/30 of 1962 in the later livery, passes on service 24 for Swarcliffe. In 1966 the abattoir was re-located in Pontefract Road, and this area is now home to a multi-storey car park and the National Express Coach Station. (*Malcolm King Collection*)

In 1966, the first 33-foot-long Daimler Fleetline (HNW 131D) was introduced. It featured panoramic windows, a wrap around windscreen and, as previously, only minimal ventilators, unusually fitted to the emergency doors and lower saloon engine bay window. Again, the Roe H45/33F bodywork had the Earls Court touches and the bus was for the first time accompanied at the 1966 show by a Leeds (Roe) AEC Swift at the same show. After being used as trainer bus no. 20, the bus was eventually purchased via the Transperience Museum by the Keighley Bus Museum Trust. (*M Berry Collection*)

This Roe-bodied Daimler Fleetline from 1966 stands ahead of a 1962 Weymann Leyland Titan outside Bramley Depot. (*Malcolm King Collection*)

Following the purchase of a solitary Roe-bodied prototype AEC Swift (GUM 951D) in 1966, these smart AEC Swifts (952–60) were supplied by Roe a year later. One of that batch, JNW 958E, passes through Gledhill.

Among the Roe products delivered were the occasional MCW buses, built to a similar design. MUG 100F (100) of 1968 vintage was one such vehicle. (*Malcolm King Collection*)

Among the last single door Leyland Atlanteans delivered to Leeds were these 78-seat PDR2/1s, delivered in 1968 and built by Park Royal. These vehicles represented the largest batch to be manufactured for the Department by that coachbuilder.

At Shadwell terminus, in a sparse covering of snow, is 7514 UA from the 1959 order of Daimler CVG6LX/30 buses. On 31 December 1976, this bus became the last rear loader vehicle to run in the city when it ran from Kirkstall to Swarcliffe. It was saved for preservation by the Leeds 514 preservation group before subsequently passing to the Keighley Bus Museum, where it is awaiting further restoration.

This varied line-up depicts the changing face of the Department in later years. From right to left are: 7525 UA, a Roe-bodied Daimler; Leyland UUA 209 in driver training colours; AEC Regent MUG 460 with full non-painted bonnet; AEC Regent V 928 CUG with the later design of un-painted hood; and finally FUB 130D from the 1966 Daimler Fleetlines in one-man livery. (*Malcolm King Collection*)

AEC Regents WUA 775 and 770 stand adjacent to JUM 220L (770), which was later renumbered 220 in the fleet. (*Malcolm King Collection*)

The new dedicated one-man, dual-door reversed livery was introduced with these 1968 Roe bodied Atlanteans (H45/33D) to a Tom Lord design. PUB 159G stands at the Hyde Park terminus, waiting for the return journey to Old Farnley. This route (49) was the first one-man-operated double-deck service for Leeds.

In its later reversed one-man livery, the twin headlights give this bus away as the ex-show bus 101 LNW from 1964 which is on the Greenthorpe (11) route at Seacroft. By this time, upper deck ventilators had been fitted due to passenger complaints.

On the 9 Ring Road service is 1962 AEC Reliance 841 CUM, with a Roe 41-seat dual-door entrance body, in the later revised livery. (*Malcolm King Collection*)

The 1966 Roe bodies on these Daimler Fleetlines were more up to date and once again the wrap around windscreen was in vogue. FUB 129D of this delivery is seen at Woodhouse Lane on the Beeston route.

The second Leyland Atlantean batch to be delivered was supplied by MCW in 1966 and built to a design used in Newcastle. These buses were to be the last 30-foot double-deckers supplied to the Department. In Wellington Street, 342 (HUA 342D) is seen on the joint Bradford service.

AEC Swift MUB 190F (90) in the one-man livery dates from 1968 and carries an MCW body. (*Malcolm King Collection*)

Looking very smart is 1009 (SUB 409G), one of fifty Park Royal bodied AEC Swifts purchased in 1969, pictured while waiting its return to the central bus station. (*Malcolm King Collection*)

Domestic Street is the scene as no. 378 from the Park Royal deliveries picks up on the 29 Middleton service. The passing Ford truck is a member of the Associated Dairy & Farms Stores Ltd, which was founded in Leeds in 1949 and later became Asda Stores in 1965.

The 33-foot-long Daimlers of 1968 introduced dual-door, one-man buses to Leeds. Another feature was the introduction of panoramic windows. The new livery reveals a stark contrast with the livery on the earlier (1964) Roe product.

Daimler Fleetline/Roe UNW 167H passes the former Fine Fare store at Crossgates en-route to Raynville, near Bramley.

Seen climbing Kirkstall Hill on the 44 Halton Moor service is UNW 176H, from the 1970 batch of Daimler Fleetline CRG6LXB vehicles. The bodywork again was a typical Roe 78-seat, dual-door layout.

In an effort to expand one man operations, Leeds bought a batch of AEC Swift single-deck buses in the late 1960s and early 1970s, together with a batch of some thirty Daimler Fleetlines. These were on SRG6LXB/36 chassis and were built by Park Royal. Of this group, 1202 (UNW 202H) stands in the Central Bus Station.

XUM 428J was another Commercial Motor Show bus by Roe in 1970. The main feature this time was the squared off wheel arches, the only bus to have this design. (*Malcolm King Collection*)

The race is on as the 1970/1 Atlantean in one-man livery takes the road to pass WUA 800, a 1956 Roe-bodied AEC Regent V, on Gelderd Road.

An interesting comparison at Leeds Bus station as Leeds ANW 464J passes Sheffield Park Royal bodied Leyland PDR2/1 YWA 122G (722), which dates from 1968. (*Malcolm King Collection*)

On the descent towards Stump Cross and Shibden, XUM 437J is seen on the 508 Leeds–Halifax service.

XUM 444J, on the 42 Harehills route, travels on Infirmary Street, Leeds, which now runs one way, contrary to this shot, and is limited access (mainly for buses).

After deliveries from Park Royal (Fleetline single-deckers) and MCW Swifts, Leeds returned to Roe to supply their last AEC Swifts in 1971. AUB 155J is seen when new. (*Malcolm King Collection*)

The Mercedes Benz L406D Shoppers' specials bought in 1971 were a new concept for the Department. These van-based vehicles were bodied by Deansgate and catered for thirteen seated passengers in a perimeter arrangement, with nine standees. YUA 530J was one of five such buses supplied.

One of the short-lived Morrison Electricars, CWO 516K, enters the bus station opposite the Quarry Hill flats on the Shoppers' Special service. (*Malcolm King Collection*)

Another demonstrator used by the Department for the Shoppers' Special service was this Seddon Pennine 4 with a twenty-five-seat DP25F body built by Seddon which came via Aberdeen Corporation. (*Malcolm King Collection*)

The 1971 deliveries from Roe were once again on Leyland Atlantean PDR2/1 chassis, with H45/33D dual-door bodywork. DUA 472K passes the former coach station on Wellington Street.

As the final day of Department operations neared, the body shop experimented with various designs for the new management's approval. DUA 485K sports one such livery. On 5 October 1978 the last bus remaining in Leeds City livery, sister Atlantean 481 (DUA 581K) was repainted in Metro colours. (*Malcolm King Collection*)

An interesting experiment carried out at Kirkstall Road Works was the dual painting for comparison notes for the new Directors. To this end, AUB 165J of the final batch of Roe-bodied AEC Swifts was the chosen vehicle. The offside of the bus was painted in the normal green with lighter relief colouring and green wheels. (*Malcolm King Collection*)

The near side of the vehicle was painted in comparatively lighter shades, red wheels with yellow entrance doors and red exit doors. (*Malcolm King Collection*)

Standing outside Kirkstall Road Works, AUB 165J displays the final version of the new livery, which differed greatly from the practices, although the red wheels and alternate coloured doors remained.

In the same livery, ANW 447J prepares to leave the bus station for Headingley while an Atlantean in Department livery can be seen in the background.

These Plaxton Elite Express bodied Leyland Leopards were latecomers to the Department which also carried the final Department crest prior to full Metro take-over. Three such vehicles were delivered in 1973 but were withdrawn within 2 years of PTE ownership.

The last bus delivered to Leeds City Transport in Department livery was SUG 591M (591) and is seen outside Charles H. Roe at Crossgates prior to delivery. The red wheels were from a PTE edict to overhaul wheels and tyres throughout the Departments. Subsequent vehicles from this batch (592 onwards) were delivered in Metro Verona green and Buttermilk. (*Malcolm King Collection*)

At the end of the line, no. 914 of the 1960 Regent V MCWs, with smashed upper saloon windows, awaits its fate alongside 945 (GUA 945), a Roe-bodied Regent V which was new in 1965 and finally scrapped in 1975 after being in PTE ownership for just twelve months. (*M. Berry Collection*)